INDEX

FIRST EDITION

1962

January

M	T	W	T	F	S	S
1	2	3	4	5	6	7
8	9	10	11	12	13	14
15	16	17	18	19	20	21
22	23	24	25	26	27	28
29	30	31				

●:6 ◐:13 ○:20 ◑:28

February

M	T	W	T	F	S	S
			1	2	3	4
5	6	7	8	9	10	11
12	13	14	15	16	17	18
19	20	21	22	23	24	25
26	27	28				

●:5 ◐:11 ○:19 ◑:27

March

M	T	W	T	F	S	S
			1	2	3	4
5	6	7	8	9	10	11
12	13	14	15	16	17	18
19	20	21	22	23	24	25
26	27	28	29	30	31	

●:6 ◐:13 ○:21 ◑:29

April

M	T	W	T	F	S	S
						1
2	3	4	5	6	7	8
9	10	11	12	13	14	15
16	17	18	19	20	21	22
23	24	25	26	27	28	29
30						

●:4 ◐:11 ○:20 ◑:27

May

M	T	W	T	F	S	S
	1	2	3	4	5	6
7	8	9	10	11	12	13
14	15	16	17	18	19	20
21	22	23	24	25	26	27
28	29	30	31			

●:4 ◐:11 ○:19 ◑:26

June

M	T	W	T	F	S	S
				1	2	3
4	5	6	7	8	9	10
11	12	13	14	15	16	17
18	19	20	21	22	23	24
25	26	27	28	29	30	

●:2 ◐:10 ○:18 ◑:25

July

M	T	W	T	F	S	S
						1
2	3	4	5	6	7	8
9	10	11	12	13	14	15
16	17	18	19	20	21	22
23	24	25	26	27	28	29
30	31					

●:2 ◐:10 ○:17 ◑:24 ●:31

August

M	T	W	T	F	S	S
		1	2	3	4	5
6	7	8	9	10	11	12
13	14	15	16	17	18	19
20	21	22	23	24	25	26
27	28	29	30	31		

◐:8 ○:15 ◑:22 ●:30

September

M	T	W	T	F	S	S
					1	2
3	4	5	6	7	8	9
10	11	12	13	14	15	16
17	18	19	20	21	22	23
24	25	26	27	28	29	30

◐:7 ○:14 ◑:20 ●:28

October

M	T	W	T	F	S	S
1	2	3	4	5	6	7
8	9	10	11	12	13	14
15	16	17	18	19	20	21
22	23	24	25	26	27	28
29	30	31				

◐:6 ○:13 ◑:20 ●:28

November

M	T	W	T	F	S	S
			1	2	3	4
5	6	7	8	9	10	11
12	13	14	15	16	17	18
19	20	21	22	23	24	25
26	27	28	29	30		

◐:5 ○:11 ◑:19 ●:27

December

M	T	W	T	F	S	S
					1	2
3	4	5	6	7	8	9
10	11	12	13	14	15	16
17	18	19	20	21	22	23
24	25	26	27	28	29	30
31						

◐:4 ○:11 ◑:18 ●:26

PEOPLE IN HIGH OFFICE

Monarch - Queen Elizabeth II
Reign: 6th February 1952 - Present
Predecessor: King George VI
Heir Apparent: Charles, Prince of Wales

United Kingdom

Prime Minister
Harold Macmillan
Conservative Party
10th January 1957 - 19th October 1963

Australia

Canada

United States

Prime Minister
Sir Robert Menzies
19th December 1949 -
26th January 1966

Prime Minister
John Diefenbaker
21st June 1957 -
22nd April 1963

President
John F. Kennedy
20th January 1961 -
22nd November 1963

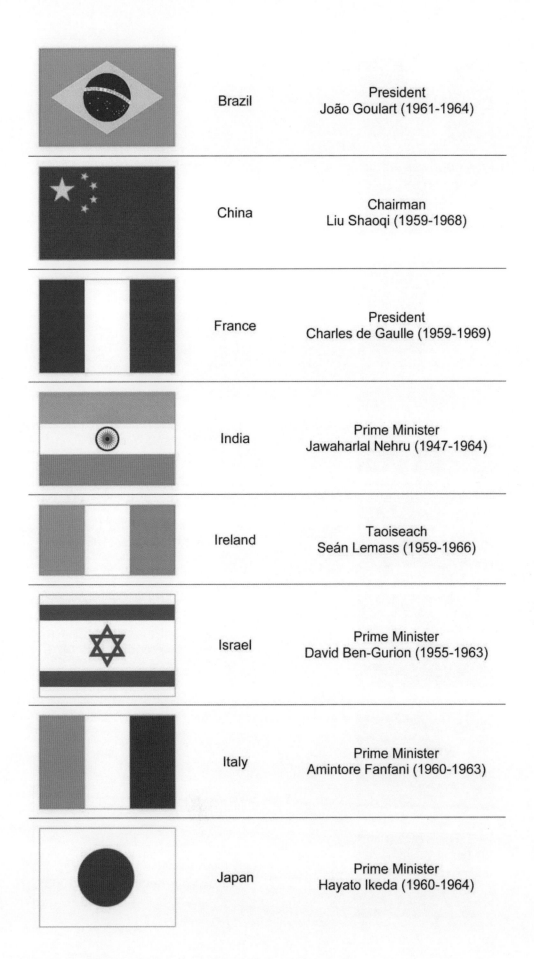

	Brazil	President João Goulart (1961-1964)
	China	Chairman Liu Shaoqi (1959-1968)
	France	President Charles de Gaulle (1959-1969)
	India	Prime Minister Jawaharlal Nehru (1947-1964)
	Ireland	Taoiseach Seán Lemass (1959-1966)
	Israel	Prime Minister David Ben-Gurion (1955-1963)
	Italy	Prime Minister Amintore Fanfani (1960-1963)
	Japan	Prime Minister Hayato Ikeda (1960-1964)

Mexico

President
Adolfo López Mateos (1958-1964)

New Zealand

Prime Minister
Keith Holyoake (1960-1972)

Pakistan

President
Ayub Khan (1958-1969)

South Africa

Prime Minister
Hendrik Verwoerd (1958-1966)

Soviet Union

Communist Party Leader
Nikita Khrushchev (1953-1964)

Spain

President
Francisco Franco (1938-1973)

Turkey

Prime Minister
İsmet İnönü (1961-1965)

West Germany

Chancellor
Konrad Adenauer (1949-1963)

BRITISH NEWS & EVENTS

January - April: An outbreak of smallpox occurs after a traveller from Pakistan arrives in Cardiff and is diagnosed with the disease. Over the following months 900,000 people are vaccinated and a huge operation is mounted to trace contacts and contain the outbreak. In total 45 people are infected and 19 die in south Wales.

2nd January: BBC Television broadcasts the first episode of the police crime drama Z-Cars. Injecting a new element of harsh realism into the image of the police, the series would run for 801 episodes until the 20th September 1978. *Photo (from left): Frank Windsor (DS John Watt), Stratford John (DCI Barlow), James Ellis (PC Bert Lynch) and Jeremy Kemp (PC Bob Steele).*

15th	Nicolai Poliakoff, aka Coco the Clown, is surprised by Eamonn Andrews for BBC televisions "This is Your Life" while appearing with the Bertram Mills circus at London's Olympia. *Fun facts: Born in Latvia, Poliakoff was arguably the most famous clown in the United Kingdom in the mid-20th century. He was appointed an OBE in 1963 by the Queen.*
18th	The Union-Castle Line ship RMS Transvaal Castle, built by John Brown & Company at Clydebank, makes her maiden voyage from Southampton to Durban, South Africa.
22nd	James Hanratty goes on trial at Bedfordshire Assizes for the A6 murder of 36-year-old Michael Gregsten and the attempted murder of Mr Gregsten's mistress Valerie Storie, who was paralysed during the attack.
24th	Brian Epstein signs a management contract with the Beatles (Paul McCartney, John Lennon, George Harrison and original drummer Pete Best). *Fun fact: In July 2019 that same contract sold for £275,000 at Sotheby's Auction House.*

| 4th | The Sunday Times becomes the first British newspaper to print a colour supplement. |

12th February: Six members of anti-war group the Committee of 100 appear at the Old Bailey in London - they face charges under the Official Secrets Act for organising the previous year's demonstration at USAF Wethersfield in Essex. *Photo (from left) Anne Randle, her husband Michael Randle, Patt Pottle, Trevor Hatton, Helen Allegranza, Ian Dixon and Terence Chandler. All except Mrs Randle were charged and sentenced to 18 months imprisonment.*

| 21st | In his debut with the Royal Ballet, Rudolf Nureyev dances with Margot Fonteyn for the first time (Giselle). *Fun facts: Despite their 19-year age difference (Nureyev was 23-years-old and Fonteyn 42) the duo immediately became an international sensation, each dancer pushing the other to their best performances. Fonteyn finally retired in 1979, aged 60, after a 17-year dancing partnership with Nureyev.* |
| 26th | The Irish Republican Army officially calls off its Border Campaign (codenamed Operation Harvest) in Northern Ireland. |

MAR

1st	British nuclear testing in the United States begins with "Pampas", Britain's first underground test at the Nevada Test Site. The tests (24 in total) continue until the 26th November 1991.
7th	The National Economic Development Council, a tripartite collaboration between government, trade unions and industrialists to address Britain's relative economic decline, first meets.
7th	An outlier of the Ash Wednesday Storm of 1962 wreaks havoc on the coastline of Cornwall, with Penzance and Newlyn bearing the brunt of the damage.
11th	Fourth Division team Accrington Stanley's resignation from the Football League (due to huge debts) is accepted by Alan Hardaker, the League Secretary.

MAR

13th	Conservative Norman Miscampbell wins the Blackpool North by-election; it is the last parliamentary by-election in England to be held on a day other than Thursday.
29th	The Education Act 1962 comes into law requiring local education authorities to pay the tuition fees of students attending full-time first-degree courses, and to provide them with a maintenance grant (superseding the former system of State Scholarships). *Follow up: The Act was repealed under the Labour government of Tony Blair in 1999, along with the introduction of tuition fees.*

APR

2nd April: The first public Panda crossing opens outside Waterloo railway station in London. The design is not a success and is subsequently replaced by the X-way (1967), and then by the modern-day pelican crossing (1969). *Photo: Ernest Marples, Minister of Transport, and A. C. Dennis, Mayor of Lambeth, are the first to use the new Panda pedestrian crossing at York Road, outside Waterloo Station.*

4th	James Hanratty is hanged at Bedford Prison for the A6 murder despite protestations from many people who believe he is innocent. *Follow up: Modern testing of DNA from Hanratty's exhumed corpse and members of his family convinced Court of Appeal judges in 2002 that Hanratty's guilt was proved "beyond doubt".*
18th	The Commonwealth Immigrants Act is given Royal assent, imposing stringent restrictions on the entry of Commonwealth citizens into Britain. Only those with work permits (typically high-skilled workers, such as doctors) are permitted entry; the Act comes into effect on the 1st July.
26th	The British Ariel 1 satellite is launched from Cape Canaveral in Florida. The launch makes the United Kingdom the third country to operate a satellite after the Soviet Union and the United States.

8th May: The final trolleybus in London runs. Its route is so thronged with sightseers and people trying to board that it does not arrive back at its final destination, Fulwell Depot, until the early hours of the 9th May. *NB: For much of its existence the London trolleybus system was the largest in the world, peaking at 68 routes with a maximum fleet of 1,811 trolleybuses. Fun facts: Trolleybuses, nicknamed "Diddlers", were first introduced in London on the 16th May 1931.*

25th	The new Coventry Cathedral is consecrated in the presence of the Queen (who had laid the foundation stone on the 23rd March 1956). Five days later the Cathedral had its musical christening with first performance of Benjamin Britten's 'War Requiem', composed especially for the occasion.
26th	Acker Bilk's 'Stranger On The Shore' becomes the first British recording to reach No.1 on the U.S. Billboard Hot 100 music chart.
31st	A general election is held in Northern Ireland. Like all previous elections to the Parliament of Northern Ireland it produces a large majority for the Ulster Unionist Party, who win 34 out of the 51 available seats.

JUN

2nd	The champions of the Southern League, Oxford United F.C., are elected to the Football League, occupying the vacant place left by bankrupt Accrington Stanley.
6th	The Beatles sign a recording contract with EMI's Parlophone record label and play their first session at Abbey Road Studios. Producer George Martin informs Brian Epstein that for future recordings he will use a session drummer in place of Pete Best.

14th June: BBC Television broadcasts the first episode of the sitcom Steptoe and Son. Written by Ray Galton and Alan Simpson, four series were broadcast by the BBC from 1962 to 1965, followed by a second run from 1970 to 1974. *NB: The first episode, The Offer, was originally broadcast as a Comedy Playhouse pilot on the 5th January 1962. Photo: Actors Harry H Corbett (Harold) and Wilfrid Brambell (Albert) pictured with their horse "Hercules" in a scene from the first episode of the television sitcom Steptoe and Son.*

29th	The British Vickers VC10 long-range jet airliner makes its maiden flight from Brooklands to Wisley.

JUL

3rd	Chichester Festival Theatre opens. Its first production is 'The Chances' by Jacobean playwright John Fletcher (1579-1625). *NB: Laurence Olivier is the theatre's inaugural artistic director.*
11th	The first live transatlantic television broadcast from the United States to Britain takes place via AT&T's Telstar 1, the world's first active, direct relay communications satellite (launched the previous day aboard a NASA Thor-Delta rocket from Cape Canaveral). *Fun facts: Telstar 1 facilitated over 400 telephone, telegraph, facsimile and television transmissions, and operated until November 1962, when its on-board electronics failed due to the effects of radiation. Although no longer functional the satellite is still in orbit to this day.*
11th	American film producer Fred Baldasare becomes the first person to swim across the English Channel underwater, without surfacing. He swims in a boat-towed cage, 15-foot below the surface, wearing a frogman outfit and breathing from oxygen tanks. The crossing takes 19 hours, 1 minute.

12th	The Rolling Stones make their debut at London's Marquee Jazz Club. The line-up is: Mick Jagger (vocals), Keith Richards & Elmo Lewis (guitars), Dick Taylor (bass), Ian Stewart (piano), and Mick Avory (drums).
13th	In what the press dubs "the Night of the Long Knives", and amid declining Conservative popularity, the Prime Minister Harold Macmillan dismisses seven members of his Cabinet, one-third of the total.

20th July: The world's first scheduled passenger hovercraft service between Wallasey, on the Wirral Peninsula, Merseyside, and Rhyl in North Wales, is introduced. Costing £2 for a return ticket, the 12-ton Vickers-Armstrong VA-3 Hovercraft, operated by British United Airways, can carry up to 24 passengers. *Follow up: The failure of one of the engines marked a premature end to the service on the 14th September 1962.*

28th	Race riots break out in Dudley, West Midlands. Dozens of white men and youths rampage in the North Street area of the town, vandalising properties in the area where the town's ethnic minorities are concentrated.
31st	Former fascist leader Sir Oswald Mosley is assaulted at a rally in London's East End. He and members of his anti-Semitic Blackshirt group are punched to the ground; the police are forced to close the meeting within three minutes and 54 people are arrested.

AUG

4th	Cymdeithas yr Iaith Gymraeg, the Welsh Language Society, is founded at Pontarddulais in South Wales.
6th	The Colony of Jamaica gains its independence from the United Kingdom after 300 years of British rule.
15th	The BMC ADO16 economy car series, best known as the Austin / Morris 1100, is launched; it becomes Britain's best-selling car for most of the 1960s.

AUG

17th	The Tornados' recording of "Telstar", written and produced by Joe Meek, is released. *Fun facts: The single reaches No.1 in both the U.K. and U.S., and is notably the first American No.1 single by a British group.*
18th	Ringo Starr officially replaces Pete Best as Beatles' drummer and they play their first live engagement with the line-up of John, Paul, George and Ringo at the Port Sunlight Horticultural Society's annual show in Birkenhead.
23rd	John Lennon marries Cynthia Powell at Mount Pleasant register office in Liverpool.
31st	Trinidad and Tobago gains its independence from the United Kingdom.
31st	Mountaineers Chris Bonington and Ian Clough become first Britons to conquer the north face of the Eiger.

SEP

1st	The ITV franchise Channel Television launches to 54,000 households in the Channel Islands.
2nd	Glasgow Corporation Tramways runs its last cars in normal service between the depots at Dalmarnock and Coplawhill, an event attended by 250,000 people. *Note: This left the Blackpool tramway as the only remaining city / town to operate trams until the opening of the Manchester Metrolink in April 1992.*
6th	Archaeologist Peter Marsden discovers the first of a set of Roman shipwrecks at Blackfriars in London (known as the Blackfriars Ships).

8th September: The famous Pines Express passenger service, operating between Manchester and Bournemouth over the Somerset and Dorset Railway line, runs for the last time. It fittingly uses the last steam locomotive built by British Railways, the BR Standard Class 9F locomotive, 92220 Evening Star.

8th	The last Gentlemen v Players cricket match is played at Scarborough (the Players win the game by 7 wickets). *Fun facts: First played in 1806, the Gentlemen v Players cricket match was a long-running series of English first-class cricket matches played between teams consisting of amateur (Gentlemen) and professional cricketers (Players). The series ended because the MCC abolished amateur status in 1963.*
14th	Wales West and North Television (Teledu Cymru) goes on air, extending ITV to the whole of the United Kingdom.
19th	Atlantic College opens its doors for the first time in Wales, marking the birth of the pioneering United World College educational movement.
19th	The first ICT 1301 business mainframe computer, "Flossie", is installed at Senate House (University of London), and is to be used for computing exam results for students. One of the first mass-produced British business computers, it weighs 5½ tons and has a footprint of around 6 x 7 meters.

21st September: Ford launches the Cortina, a family saloon costing £580. Aimed at buyers of the Morris Oxford Farina and Vauxhall Victor, the car was designed to be economical to buy, cheap to run, and easy and inexpensive to produce. *Fun facts: The Cortina was built in various guises from 1962 to 1982, and was the Britain's' best-selling car of the 1970s; a total of more than 2.8 million were sold in the U.K. during its 20-year five-generation production run.*

21st	Granada Television's University Challenge airs for the first time, with Bamber Gascoigne as its quizmaster.
28th	Barrister Elizabeth Lane becomes the first female County Court judge and is sworn in at the House of Lords. *NB: Three years later Lane becomes the first woman to sit in the High Court and is appointed a Dame Commander of the Most Excellent Order of the British Empire (corresponding to the customary knighthood received on appointment by a male High Court judge).*

1st October: Brian Epstein signs a second contract to manage Beatles, replacing the earlier contract which had been signed by the group's former drummer Pete Best. *Photo: Epstein with the Beatles at the premiere of A Hard Day's Night, 6th July 1964.*

5th	The first James Bond film, Dr No, premieres at the London Pavilion. Based on the novel by Ian Fleming, it stars Sean Connery and Ursula Andress.
5th	The Beatles release their first single in their own right, Love Me Do. It peaks at No.17 in the U.K. Charts and later reaches No.1 in the United States, Australia and New Zealand. *Fun fact: The first time the group's name appeared on a record was with the release of My Bonnie / The Saints (5th January 1962) which was credited to Tony Sheridan and the Beatles.*
9th	Uganda gains its independence from the United Kingdom.
17th	The Beatles make their first televised appearance, on Granada television's local news programme People and Places. They sing two songs: Some Other Guy, and their new single, Love Me Do.
21st	The first American Folk Blues Festival plays its only U.K. date at the Free Trade Hall, Manchester; artists include Sonny Terry, Brownie McGhee and T-Bone Walker. *Notes: The tour attracted substantial media coverage and became influential on the British R&B scene; audience members at the show included Mick Jagger, Keith Richards, Brian Jones and Jimmy Page.*
24th	GCHQ's interception station at Scarborough is the first to detect that Soviet merchant ships, implicated in the Cuban Missile Crisis, were turning around and heading back to the Soviet Union.

NOV

	Orthopaedic surgeon Professor John Charnley makes the world's first successful whole hip replacement operation at Wrightington Hospital, Wigan.

NOV

17th	During a rescue the life-boat George Elmy is capsized by two huge waves just 30 yards from Seaham Harbour's South Pier in east Durham. The tragedy claims the lives of the five volunteer crew members and four of five fishermen who had just been rescued.
22nd	The 7th British Empire and Commonwealth Games open in Perth, Australia.
24th	The first episode of influential satirical comedy show "That Was the Week That Was", hosted by David Frost, is broadcast on BBC Television.
29th	An agreement is signed between Britain and France to develop the Concorde supersonic airliner.

DEC

4th	A severe smog lasting 3 days leads to the deaths of an estimated 300-700 people across Greater London. *Note: The 1962 London smog occurred ten years after the Great Smog of London, in which serious air pollution killed as many as 12,000 people and had led to the passing of the 1956 Clean Air Act.*
6th	The last native inhabitants of the Scottish Island of Stroma leave bringing to an end thousands of years of permanent habitation on the island.
7th	The Atlas supercomputer is dedicated at the University of Manchester. *NB: Considered to be the most powerful computer in the world at that time, it remained in use until it was eventually shut down on the 30th November 1971.*
8th	An attempted coup takes place in the British protectorate of Brunei by opponents of its monarchy and its proposed inclusion in the Federation of Malaysia.
9th	Tanganyika (modern-day Tanzania) becomes a republic within the Commonwealth, with Julius Nyerere as president.
10th	British molecular biologists Francis Crick and Maurice Wilkins, along with American James D. Watson, win the Nobel Prize in Physiology or Medicine for their work in determining the structure of DNA.
10th	British biochemists Max Perutz and John Cowdery Kendrew win the Nobel Prize in Chemistry for their work investigating the structure of haemoglobin and myoglobin.
10th	David Lean's epic film Lawrence of Arabia, based on life of T. E. Lawrence and starring Peter O'Toole, Omar Sharif, Alec Guinness, Jack Hawkins and Anthony Quinn, premieres in London (Academy Awards Best Picture 1963).
21st	Nassau Agreement: Britain agrees to buy the Polaris submarine-launched ballistic missile system from the United States.
22nd	The "Big Freeze" hits Britain in what will be the coldest Winter since 1895. *NB: There would not be another frost-free morning again until the 6th March 1963.*
29th	Graham Hill wins the South African Grand Prix (to take the first of his two F1 World Drivers Championships) by 12 points from Jim Clark.

99 WORLDWIDE NEWS & EVENTS

1. 1st January: Western Samoa gains its independence from New Zealand.
2. 8th January: Harmelen train disaster: Ninety-three people are killed in the worst railway accident in the history of the Netherlands.
3. 8th January: Twenty-one-year-old future Hall of Fame golfer Jack Nicklaus makes his first professional appearance at the Los Angeles Open; Nicklaus finishes in a tie for 50th place, netting him a grand total of $33.33 in prize money.
4. 10th January: A massive avalanche on Huascarán, Peru's highest mountain in the Andes range, totally destroys the entire town of Ranrahirca along with eight other villages; an estimated 4,000 people are believed to have been killed.
5. 12th January: America's first major combat mission in the Vietnam War, Operation Chopper, begins.
6. 28th January: Johannes Relleke is stung 2,443 times by bees at the Kamativi tin mine in the Wankie District of Zimbabwe (then Rhodesia). Relleke amazingly survives; all the stings are removed and counted.
7. 31st January: The Organization of American States suspends Cuba's membership; the suspension is lifted 47 years later on the 3rd June 2009.
8. 4th February: A rare grand conjunction of the Sun, Moon, Mercury, Venus, Mars, Jupiter and Saturn occurs (all of them within 16° of one another).
9. 7th February: A methane explosion occurs at the Luisenthal Coal Mine in Saarland, West Germany; 299 of the 433 workers present are killed.
10. 9th February: The Taiwan Stock Exchange opens for the first time.

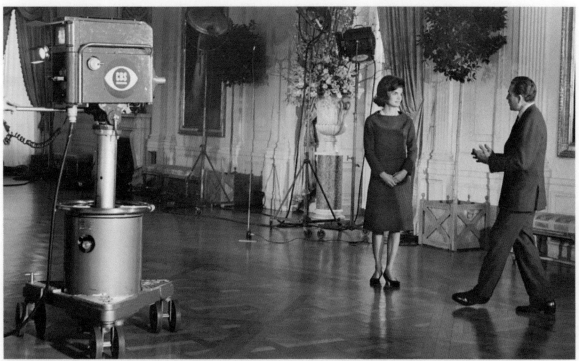

11. 14th February: America's First Lady Jacqueline Kennedy takes television viewers on a tour of the recently renovated White House. Broadcast across the United States, the documentary is seen by more than eighty million viewers and is syndicated globally to 50 countries, including China and the Soviet Union.

12.	16th February: Heavy storms flood Germany's North Sea coast, mainly around Hamburg; 315 people die and 60,000 lose their homes.
13.	20th February: Project Mercury: John Glenn, aboard the Mercury-Atlas 6 spacecraft Friendship 7, becomes the first American to orbit the Earth. Glenn completes three orbits in 4 hours 55 minutes before re-entering the Earth's atmosphere and splashing down in the North Atlantic Ocean.
14.	27th February: South Vietnam President Ngô Đình Diệm's palace is bombed by two dissident Republic of Vietnam Air Force pilots in a failed assassination attempt.
15.	2nd March: General Ne Win seizes power in Burma in a coup d'état.
16.	5th March: The 19th Golden Globe Awards, honouring the best in film for 1961, are held at the Beverly Hilton Hotel in Beverly Hills, California. The winners include the epic adventure war film The Guns of Navarone, Maximilian Schell and Geraldine Page.
17.	12th March: The Titan II rocket makes its first flight from Cape Canaveral, Florida, flying some 5,000 miles downrange and depositing its re-entry vehicle in the Ascension Island splash net. *Notes: Titan II was originally designed and used as an intercontinental ballistic missile (ICBM), but was later adapted as a medium-lift space launch vehicle to carry payloads to Earth orbit for the U.S. Air Force, NASA and the National Oceanic and Atmospheric Administration.*
18.	18th March: France and the Provisional Government of the Algerian Republic sign an agreement in Évian-les-Bains, France. The "Évian Accords" formally end the Algerian War (1954-1962).
19.	18th March: In Luxembourg Isabelle Aubret wins the 7th Eurovision Song Contest for France with the song "Un Premier Amour"; it is France's third victory in the contest in just five years. *Fun facts: Austria, Belgium, Netherlands and Spain all score the infamous nul points - the United Kingdom's Ronnie Carroll comes 4th singing "Ring-A-Ding Girl".*
20.	19th March: Bob Dylan, often regarded as one of the greatest songwriters of all time, releases his self-titled debut studio album.
21.	21st March: In the United States the Taco Bell fast food restaurant chain is founded by Glen Bell. *Fun facts: Today, Taco Bell serves over two billion customers each year and has over 7,000 restaurants around the world.*
22.	21st March: A two-year-old female black bear named "Yogi" is ejected from 35,000 feet (10,700 meters) by a U.S. Air Force Convair B-58 Hustler during tests of the Hustler's escape capsule. Yogi, the first creature to be ejected at supersonic speeds by the U.S. military, survives the test and lands unharmed 7 minutes, 49 seconds later. *NB: Yogi is later euthanised so that doctors can examine internal organs for signs of damage.*
23.	23rd March: The Scandinavian States of the Nordic Council (Denmark, Finland, Iceland, Norway and Sweden) sign the Helsinki Convention on Nordic Co-operation. *NB: The Treaty enters into force on the 1st July 1962.*
24.	April: The first computer video game "Spacewar" (developed by Steve Russell in collaboration with Martin Graetz, Wayne Wiitanen, Bob Saunders, Steve Piner, and others) is written for the newly installed DEC PDP-1 minicomputer at the Massachusetts Institute of Technology.
25.	2nd April: Jawaharlal Nehru's Indian National Congress party wins a landslide victory and he is elected Prime Minister of India for the fourth time.
26.	9th April: The 34th Academy Awards ceremony, honouring the best in film for 1961, is hosted by Bob Hope in Santa Monica, California. The winners include West Side Story (10 awards), Sophia Loren and Maximilian Schell.

27. | 14th April: Future French President Georges Pompidou becomes Prime Minister of France after the resignation of Michel Debré.

28. 21st April: In the United States the Century 21 Exposition World's Fair is opened by exposition president Joseph Gandy in Seattle, Washington. The theme for the Fair centres on modern science, space exploration and the progressive future. It sees the construction of the 605-foot (184 meters) Space Needle and Alweg monorail, as well as several sports venues and performing arts buildings. The exposition gives Seattle world-wide recognition and by the time it closes on the 21st October 1962, it has been officially visited by 9,609,969 people. *Photos: The top of The Space Needle / Aerial view of an avenue at the World's Fair.*

29. | 24th April: The robotic spacecraft Ranger 4 is launched from Cape Canaveral in Florida toward the Moon. *Fun fact: Although Ranger 4 failed in its mission to transmit pictures of the lunar surface before it crashed onto the far side of the Moon two days later, it did acquire the honour of being the first U.S. spacecraft to reach another celestial body.*

30. | 24th April: The Massachusetts Institute of Technology sends the first television image transmitted by communication satellite. It is sent via the Echo I balloon satellite, 2,700 miles from Camp Parks, California to Westford, Massachusetts.

31. | 29th April: The 16th Tony Awards take place in the Waldorf-Astoria Grand Ballroom in New York City. The winners include Robert Bolt's play A Man For All Seasons, Paul Scofield and Margaret Leighton.

32. | 2nd May: Benfica win the European Cup for the second time after beating Real Madrid 5-3 in front of 61,257 fans at the Olympisch Stadion in Amsterdam.

33. | 3rd May: A freight train and two passenger trains collide near Mikawashima Station in Arakawa, Tokyo, Japan; 160 people are killed and 296 injured.

34. | 5th May: The soundtrack to the 1961 film West Side Story, featuring music by Leonard Bernstein and lyrics by Stephen Sondheim, reaches No.1 on the American Billboard album chart; it stays at No.1 for 54 weeks, giving it the longest chart-topping run of any album in history.

35. | 6th May: After several ballots Antonio Segni is elected as the fourth President of Italy.

36.	7th - 23rd May: The 15th Cannes Film Festival is held in Cannes, France. The Brazilian drama film "O Pagador de Promessas" (Keeper of Promises), directed by Anselmo Duarte, wins the Palme d'Or.
37.	8th May: Oskar Schindler is honoured for saving 1200 Jews during WWII in a ceremony on the Avenue of the Righteous in Jerusalem.
38.	14th May: Juan Carlos, Prince of Asturias, and Princess Sophia of Greece and Denmark, are married in Athens. *Follow up: Juan Carlos and Sophia, who now goes by Sofía (the Spanish spelling of her name), reigned as King and Queen of Spain from 1975 until his abdication in 2014.*
39.	23rd May: Construction begins on the Montreal Metro in Canada. *Fun fact: Today the Montreal Metro is North America's fourth busiest rapid transit system behind the New York City Subway, the Mexico City Metro, and the Toronto Subway, delivering an average of 1,367,200 daily passenger trips per weekday (Q4, 2018).*
40.	23rd May: Ex-General Raoul Salan, formerly the most decorated soldier in the French Army, is sentenced to life imprisonment for treason. *Notes: Salan was the founder of the extremist Organisation Armée Secrete (OAS), an organisation which carried out terrorist attacks, including bombings and assassinations, in an attempt to prevent Algeria's independence from French colonial rule; he was pardoned in 1968.*
41.	24th May: Project Mercury: Scott Carpenter, in the Aurora 7 space capsule, becomes the second American to orbit the Earth, and the fourth American in space after Alan Shepard, Gus Grissom, and John Glenn.
42.	29th May: The 4th Annual Grammy Awards, recognising accomplishments of musicians in 1961, are held at Chicago, Los Angeles and New York. The winners include Henry Mancini for "Moon River", and Judy Garland for "Judy at Carnegie Hall".
43.	30th May: The 1962 FIFA World Cup begins in Chile.
44.	1st June: Nazi war criminal Adolf Eichmann is hanged at a prison in Ramla, Israel; his body is cremated and his ashes scattered over the Mediterranean.
45.	3rd June: Air France Flight 007, a charter flight carrying cultural and civic leaders from the American city of Atlanta, Georgia, overruns the runway at Orly Airport in Paris; 130 of the 132 people on board are killed.
46.	11th June: Brothers John and Clarence Anglin, and fellow inmate Frank Morris, escape from Alcatraz Federal Penitentiary aboard an improvised inflatable raft. *Notes: The only inmates to ever escape from the maximum-security facility, no conclusive evidence has ever surfaced favouring the success or failure of the attempt. In 1979 the FBI officially concluded that the men drowned in the frigid waters of San Francisco Bay before reaching the mainland. However, the U.S. Marshals Service case file remains open and active, and Morris, and the Anglin brothers remain on its wanted list.*
47.	17th June: Brazil beats Czechoslovakia 3-1, to win the 1962 FIFA World Cup at the Estadio Nacional in Santiago, Chile.
48.	22nd June: Air France Flight 117 crashes during bad weather in Guadeloupe, West Indies, killing all 113 on board.
49.	22nd June - 3rd July: The 12th Berlin International Film Festival is held in West Berlin, Germany. The Golden Bear is awarded to the British film "A Kind of Loving" directed by John Schlesinger.
50.	1st July: Rwanda and Burundi gain their independence from Belgium.
51.	1st July: An independence referendum held in Algeria sees supporters of Algerian independence win a 99.72% majority; the voter turnout is 91.88%. *Notes: Charles de Gaulle accepts Algerian independence on the 3rd July, and Algeria becomes independent from France on the 5th July.*

52.	2nd July: American businessman and entrepreneur Sam Walton opens the first Wal-Mart store in Rogers, Arkansas. *Fun facts: Today Walmart is the world's largest company by revenue ($548.743 billion, 2020) and has 10,526 stores and clubs in 24 countries, operating under 48 different names. It is also the largest private employer in the world with 2.2 million employees.*
53.	5th - 7th July: The mass killing of Pied-Noir and European expatriates living in Algeria, by members of the Algerian National Liberation Army, takes place in Oran; estimates of the total number of people killed vary between 95 and 365.
54.	6th July: Gay Byrne presents the first edition of The Late Late Show on RTÉ in the Republic of Ireland; Byrne goes on to present the show for the next 37 years.
55.	9th July: Artist Andy Warhol premieres his Campbell's Soup Cans exhibit at the Ferus Gallery in Los Angeles, California.
56.	14th July: Norma Nolan of Argentina is crowned Miss Universe 1962 at Miami Beach in Florida.
57.	15th July: Defending champion Jacques Anquetil of France claims his 3rd Tour victory at the 49th Tour de France.

58. 17th July: Major Robert M. White flies the hypersonic rocket-powered X-15 aircraft to an altitude of 314,750 feet (59.6 miles) earning him his U.S. Air Force astronaut wings. *Fun facts: White reaches a speed of 3,831 mph during the feat and becomes the first "winged" astronaut (and one of only a few) to have flown into space without a conventional spacecraft. Photo: Test pilot Bob White pictured with a North American X-15 on Rogers Dry Lake in California on the 7th February 1961.*

59.	23rd July: The International Agreement on the Neutrality of Laos is signed by 14 states in Geneva.
60.	31st July: An annular solar eclipse occurs. The eclipse is a part of Saros cycle 135, repeating every 18 years and 11 days.

61. 4th August: Thirty-six-year-old Marilyn Monroe is found dead from an overdose of sleeping pills and chloral hydrate at her home in Brentwood, Los Angeles. Her death is officially ruled a probable suicide, although the exact cause has been disputed. *Notes: An actress, model and singer famous for playing comedic "blonde bombshell" characters, Monroe became one of the most popular sex symbols of the 1950s and early 1960s, and was emblematic of the era's sexual revolution. Long after her death she continues to be a major icon of pop culture. In 1999, the American Film Institute ranked Monroe sixth on its list of the greatest female screen legends from the Golden Age of Hollywood. Photos: A 20-year-old Marilyn Monroe before starting her film career in 1946 / Marilyn Monroe just weeks before her death in 1962.*

62.	5th August: Nelson Mandela is arrested by the South African government and charged with inciting workers' strikes, and leaving the country without permission; he is sentenced to five years imprisonment. *NB: On the 12th June 1964 Mandela is further convicted of four counts of sabotage and conspiracy to violently overthrow the government, and is sentenced to life imprisonment. Mandela serves 27 years in prison before he is released by President F. W. de Klerk in 1990. Follow up: Mandela and de Klerk led efforts to negotiate an end to apartheid, which resulted in the 1994 multiracial general election in which Mandela led the ANC to victory and became president of South Africa.*
63.	16th August: Algeria joins the Arab League.
64.	17th August: In plain view of hundreds of witnesses, East German border guards shoot 18-year-old Peter Fechter as he attempts to cross the Berlin Wall into West Berlin. Despite his screams, Fechter receives no medical assistance and bleeds to death approximately one hour later.
65.	18th August: Norway enters the space age as it launches its first sounding rocket "Ferdinand 1" from Andøya Space Center.
66.	22nd August: French Air Force lieutenant-colonel Jean Bastien-Thiry and three co-conspirators attempt to assassinate President Charles de Gaulle. *NB: For his part in the attempt Bastien-Thiry is executed by firing squad; he is the last person to be executed in this manner in France.*

67. 25th August - 8th September: The 23rd Venice International Film Festival is held in Venice, Italy. "Family Diary" directed by Valerio Zurlini, and "Ivan's Childhood" directed by Andrei Tarkovsky, are jointly awarded the Golden Lion.

68. 27th August: NASA launches the Mariner 2 Venus space probe from Cape Canaveral in Florida. An exact copy of unsuccessful Mariner 1, it becomes the first robotic space probe to conduct a successful planetary encounter. *Notes: Its closest approach to Venus (21,607 miles) was made on the 14th December 1962.*

69. 27th August - 1st September: Typhoon Wanda strikes Hong Kong leaving 434 people dead and 72,000 homeless.

70. 1st September: An earthquake in Qazvin Province, Iran, destroys over 21,000 houses and results in 12,225 fatalities.

71. 12th September: President John F. Kennedy delivers a speech at Rice University in Houston, Texas, to persuade the American people to support the Apollo program, the national effort to land a man on the Moon. In front of a crowd of around 40,000 Kennedy famously proclaims "We choose to go to the moon in this decade and do the other things, not because they are easy, but because they are hard." *NB: Kennedy's goal was realised posthumously in July 1969 with the success of the Apollo 11 mission. Photo: President Kennedy speaking at Rice University on the 12th September 1962.*

72. 17th September: NASA announce the selection of Astronaut Group 2, 9 new astronauts to augment the original Mercury Seven. *NB: The nine astronauts selected are Neil Armstrong, Frank Borman, Pete Conrad, Jim Lovell, James McDivitt, Elliot See, Tom Stafford, Ed White and John Young.*

73.	25th September: Heavyweight challenger Sonny Liston KOs Floyd Patterson in 2 minutes, 6 seconds of the first round at Comiskey Park, Chicago, to win the WBA, NYSAC, and The Ring world heavyweight boxing titles.
74.	25th September: A flash flood in Rubí, near Barcelona in Spain, kills an estimated 800 people.
75.	28th September: In Brisbane, Australia, a fire destroys the Paddington tram depot and 67 trams (20% of the city's fleet). It is one of the largest fires in Brisbane's history.
76.	29th September: The Canadian Alouette 1, the first satellite built outside the United States and the Soviet Union, is launched from Vandenberg Air Force Base in California.
77.	1st October: Twenty-year-old Barbra Streisand signs with Columbia Records (her first recording contract). *Fun facts: With a career spanning over six decades and record sales in excess of 150 million units, Streisand is one of the best-selling recording artists of all time. She has achieved success in multiple fields of entertainment and her accolades include two Academy Awards, ten Grammy Awards, five Emmy Awards, four Peabody Awards, nine Golden Globes and the Presidential Medal of Freedom.*
78.	1st October: James Meredith becomes the first African-American student to enrol at the University of Mississippi. *NB: Meredith's admission is regarded as a pivotal moment in the history of civil rights in the United States.*
79.	3rd October: Project Mercury: Walter Schirra orbits the Earth six times in the Sigma 7 space capsule to become the fifth American, and ninth human, to travel into space. *Fun Facts: Schirra was the first astronaut to go into space three times, and was the only astronaut to have flown in the Mercury, Gemini, and Apollo programs.*
80.	8th October: Algeria is accepted as the 109th member of the United Nations.
81.	8th October: In the North Korean parliamentary election Kim Il-sung's Workers' Party receives 100% of the votes; voter turnout is also reportedly 100%.
82.	11th October: Second Vatican Council: Pope John XXIII convenes the first ecumenical council of the Roman Catholic Church in 92 years.
83.	14th October: Cuban Missile Crisis: Photographs taken by a high-altitude U-2 spy plane offer incontrovertible evidence that Soviet-made medium-range missiles (capable of carrying nuclear warheads) are stationed 90 miles off the American coastline in Cuba. Two days after the pictures are taken they are presented to President Kennedy who enacts a naval blockade around Cuba. Kennedy makes it clear the U.S. is prepared to use military force if necessary to neutralise what it believes is a threat to its national security. The news leads to many people fearing the world is on the brink of a nuclear war.
84.	20th October – 21st November: The Sino-Indian War, a border dispute involving India and the People's Republic of China, begins.
85.	25th October: Uganda is admitted as the 110th member of the United Nations.
86.	27th October: Cuban Missile Crisis: After much deliberation between the Soviet Union and the United States the crisis comes to an end when Soviet leader Nikita Khrushchev offers to remove the Cuban missiles in exchange for the U.S. promising not to invade Cuba. *Notes: In a secret deal between Kennedy and Khrushchev, Kennedy agrees to the withdrawal of U.S. missiles from Turkey. The fact that this deal is not made public makes it appear that the Soviets have backed down.*
87.	1st November: The comic book antihero Diabolik first appears in Italy. *Notes: Having sold more than 150 million copies worldwide to date, Diabolik is one of the best-known and best-selling comic book series to have appeared from Europe.*

88. 3rd November: John W. Mauchly records the first ever use of the term "personal computer" in a New York Times article entitled "Pocket Computer may replace Shopping List."

89. 5th November: A coal mining disaster at Ny-Ålesund in Svalbard, Norway, kills 21 people. *Follow up: The Norwegian government is forced to resign in the aftermath of this accident (28th August 1963).*

90. 6th November: The United Nations General Assembly passes Resolution 1761 condemning South Africa's racist apartheid policies and calls for all UN member states to cease military and economic relations with the nation.

91. 8th November: At the 12th Miss World pageant held at the Lyceum Ballroom in London, England, Catharina Lodders of the Netherlands is elected Miss World 1962. *Fun fact: Lodders went on to marry American singer and dancer Chubby Checker on the 12th April 1964.*

92. 30th November: The United Nations General Assembly elects U Thant of Burma, as the new Secretary-General of the United Nations.

93. 2nd December: Vietnam War: After a trip to Vietnam, at the request of President John F. Kennedy, Senate Majority Leader Mike Mansfield reports that U.S. money given to Ngo Dinh Diem's government is being squandered and that the U.S. should avoid further involvement in Vietnam. *NB: Mansfield becomes the first American official to comment even mildly negatively on the war's condition.*

94. 10th December: American Linus Pauling is awarded the Nobel Peace Prize "for his fight against the nuclear arms race between East and West"; Pauling is one of only four individuals to have won more than one Nobel Prize - he also won the Nobel Prize in Chemistry in 1954.

95. 11th December: The last execution in Canada, the double hanging of Arthur Lucas and Ronald Turpin, is carried out at Toronto's Don Jail.

96. 14th December: Leonardo da Vinci's early 16th century painting the "Mona Lisa" is assessed for insurance purposes at $100 million (equivalent to $884 million in 2021) before touring the United States for several months; it is the highest insurance value for a painting in history.

97. 18th December: Dukler Prague midfielder Josef Masopust wins the Ballon d'Or award for best European football player; Benfica striker Eusébio is second, and FC Köln defender Karl-Heinz Schnellinger is third.

98. 24th December: The last 1,113 participants in the Bay of Pigs Invasion are returned to the U.S. after the American government agrees to a ransom of $53 million in food and medical supplies to Cuba.

99. 28th December: At the 51st Davis Cup, Australia beats Mexico 5-0 in Brisbane.

BIRTHS

British Personalities

BORN IN 1962

Gavin Hastings, OBE
b. 3rd January 1962

Rugby union player who represented
Scotland 61 times (20 times as captain).

Brian Moore
b. 11th January 1962

Rugby union player who represented
England 64 times, presenter and pundit.

Eddie Izzard
b. 7th February 1962

Stand-up comedian, actor, writer and
activist.

Hugh Dennis
b. 13th February 1962

Comedian, presenter, actor, writer,
impressionist and voice-over artist.

Vanessa Feltz
b. 21st February 1962

Television personality, broadcaster and journalist.

Craig & Charlie Reid
b. 5th March 1962

Scottish rock duo (The Proclaimers).

Clare Grogan
b. 17th March 1962

Actress and singer (Altered Images).

Sir **Steve Redgrave**, CBE, DL
b. 23rd March 1962

Rower who won gold medals at five consecutive Olympic Games (1984-2000).

Richard Coles, FRSA, FKC
b. 26th March 1962

Musician, journalist and Church of England parish priest.

Phillip Schofield
b. 1st April 1962

Television presenter.

Evan Davis
b. 8th April 1962

Economist, journalist and BBC presenter.

Nick Kamen
b. 15th April 1962
d. 5th May 2021

Singer, songwriter, musician and model.

Jimmy White, MBE
b. 2nd May 1962

Snooker player who is a six-time World
Championship finalist.

Neil Foster
b. 6th May 1962

Cricketer who played 29 Test matches and
48 One Day Internationals for England.

Paul Heaton
b. 9th May 1962

Singer-songwriter (The Housemartins,
The Beautiful South).

Dave Gahan
b. 9th May 1962

Singer-songwriter (Depeche Mode).

Perry Fenwick
b. 29th May 1962

Actor best known for playing Billy Mitchell in the BBC soap opera EastEnders.

Carol Kirkwood
b. 29th May 1962

BBC weather presenter.

Susannah Constantine
b. 3rd June 1962

Fashion guru, journalist, advisor, television presenter, author, designer and actress.

Nick Rhodes
b. 8th June 1962

Musician, singer and producer (Duran Duran).

Phill Jupitus
b. 25th June 1962

Stand-up comedian, actor, performance poet, cartoonist and podcaster.

Michael Ball, OBE
b. 27th June 1962

Singer, presenter and actor.

Neil Morrissey, MBE
b. 4th July 1962

Actor, voice actor, singer and businessman.

Andy Green, OBE
b. 30th July 1962

Royal Air Force fighter pilot and World Land
Speed Record holder.

Alexander Litvinenko
b. 30th August 1962
d. 23rd November 2006
British-naturalised Russian defector and
former Russian FSB officer.

Sir **Keir Starmer**, KCB, QC
b. 2nd September 1962

Politician, Labour Party Leader and former
lawyer.

Peter Wingfield
b. 5th September 1962

Television actor and medical doctor.

John Fashanu
b. 18th September 1962

Television presenter and former
professional footballer.

Nick Knowles
b. 21st September 1962

Television presenter, writer and musical artist.

Ally McCoist, MBE
b. 24th September 1962

Footballer who represented Scotland 61 times, manager and pundit.

Tracey Thorn
b. 26th September 1962

Singer, songwriter and writer (Everything but the Girl).

Caron Keating
b. 5th October 1962
d. 13th April 2004
Television presenter.

Micky Flanagan
b. 7th October 1962

Comedian, writer, presenter and actor.

Nick Hancock
b. 25th October 1962

Actor and television presenter.

Cary Elwes
b. 26th October 1962

Actor and writer.

Sharron Davies, MBE
b. 1st November 1962

Olympic swimmer and television presenter.

Jacqui Smith
b. 3rd November 1962

Broadcaster and former Labour politician who was the first female Home Secretary.

Alan Smith
b. 21st November 1962

Footballer who represented England 13 times, commentator and pundit.

Colin Salmon
b. 6th December 1962

Actor.

Ralph Fiennes
b. 22nd December 1962

Actor, film producer, director and an ambassador for UNICEF UK.

Notable British Deaths

16th Jan	Richard Henry "Harry" Tawney (b. 30th November 1880) - Economic historian, social critic, ethical socialist, Christian socialist and an important proponent of adult education.
24th Jan	Stanley Phillip Lord (b. 13th September 1877) - Captain of the SS Californian, the nearest ship to the Titanic on the night it sank on the 15th April 1912. *NB: The Californian was criticised for not rendering timely assistance to the Titanic despite being only 20 miles away and being the only ship that could have reached Titanic before it sank.*
26th Jan	George Jeffreys (b. 28th February 1889) - Evangelist who founded the Elim Pentecostal Church.
10th Feb	William Norman Birkett, 1st Baron Birkett, PC (b. 6th September 1883) - Barrister, judge, politician and preacher who served as the alternate British judge during the Nuremberg Trials.
13th Feb	Edward Hugh John Neale Dalton, Baron Dalton, PC (b. 16th August 1887) - Labour Party economist and politician who served as Chancellor of the Exchequer (1945-1947).
20th Feb	Herbert Halliwell Hobbes (b. 16th November 1877) - Film, television and stage actor who appeared in over 100 films.
16th Mar	Frederick Beaconsfield Pentland (b. 29th July 1883) - Football player and international coach who was capped five times for England in 1909.
23rd Mar	Edward Clement Davies, QC (b. 19th February 1884) - Politician and leader of the Liberal Party (1945-1956).
4th Apr	James Hanratty (b. 4th October 1936) - Murderer who was one of the last people in the United Kingdom to be executed.

10th April: Stuart Fergusson Victor Sutcliffe (b. 23rd June 1940) - Scottish painter and musician better known as the original bass guitarist of the Beatles. Sutcliffe left the Beatles to pursue a career as a painter in July 1961, and enrolled in the Hamburg College of Art, studying under future pop artist Eduardo Paolozzi.

Sutcliffe, who had been suffering from intense headaches and experiencing acute light sensitivity, died of a brain haemorrhage on the way to hospital after collapsing in Hamburg.

19th Apr	Sir Harold Edgar Yarrow, 2nd Baronet, CBE, FRS, FRSE (b. 11th August 1884) - Industrialist and shipbuilder who served two terms as President of the Institution of Engineers and Shipbuilders in Scotland.
21st Apr	Sir Frederick Handley Page, CBE, FRAeS (b. 15th November 1885) - Aeronautical engineer known as the father of the heavy bomber.
5th May	George Ernest Tyldesley (b. 5th February 1889) - Cricketer who played in 14 Tests for England (1921-1929) and is Lancashire's most prolific run-getter of all time. *Fun fact: Tyldesley is one of just 25 batsmen to have scored over 100 centuries in the first-class game.*

15th May	Laurence Michael Dillon (b. Laura Maud Dillon; 1st May 1915) - Physician who was the first transsexual man to undergo phalloplasty.
2nd Jun	Victoria Mary "Vita" Sackville-West, Lady Nicolson, CH (b. 9th March 1892) - Novelist, poet and journalist.
9th Jun	Henry Kendall (b. 28th May 1897) - Stage and film actor, theatre director and officer in the Royal Flying Corps (1916-1919).
12th Jun	John Nicholson Ireland (b. 13th August 1879) - Composer and teacher of music.
18th Jun	George Jonathan Sargent (b. 2nd August 1882) - Professional golfer who won the 1909 U.S. Open setting a new 72-hole scoring record for the tournament of 290. Sargent became a member of the Professional Golfers' Association of America at its inception in 1916, and served as its president for five years (1921-1926).
21st Jul	George Macaulay Trevelyan, OM, CBE, FRS, FBA (b. 16th February 1876) - Historian, academic and author.
27th Jul	Richard Aldington (b. 8th July 1892) - Writer and poet, born Edward Godfree Aldington, who was an early associate of the Imagist movement.
29th Jul	Sir Ronald Aylmer Fisher, FRS (b. 17th February 1890) - Statistician, geneticist and academic. For his work in statistics, he has been described as "a genius who almost single-handedly created the foundations for modern statistical science" and "the single most important figure in 20th century statistics".
5th Aug	John Alexander Scott Coutts (b. 9th December 1902) - Artist, fetish photographer, editor and publisher better known by the pseudonym John Willie.
15th Aug	Robert MacGregor McIntyre (b. 28th November 1928) - Motorcycle racer remembered for his five Grand Prix wins (which included three wins at the Isle of Man TT races), and for his four victories in the North West 200.
7th Sep	Graham William Walker (b. 4th August 1896) - Motorcycle racer, broadcaster and journalist.
9th Sep	Sir Geoffrey Le Mesurier Mander (b. 6th March 1882) - Midland industrialist, art collector and Liberal parliamentarian.
23rd Sep	Anthony Walter Patrick Hamilton (b. 17th March 1904) - Playwright and novelist.
4th Oct	Elias Henry Hendren (b. 5th February 1889) - Cricketer known as Patsy Hendren who played for Middlesex and England (51 Tests, 1920-1935).
21st oct	Hugh Arthur Franklin (b. 27th May 1889) - Suffragist and politician. Born into a wealthy Anglo-Jewish family, Franklin rejected both his religious and social upbringing to protest for women's suffrage.
3rd Nov	Ralph Hodgson (b. 9th September 1871) - Georgian poet who was awarded the Queen's Gold Medal for Poetry (1954).
5th Nov	Percy Cudlipp (b. 10th November 1905) - Prominent Welsh journalist.
15th Dec	Charles Laughton (b. 1st July 1899) - Stage and film actor who won the Academy Award for Best Actor in The Private Life of Henry VIII (1933).
21st Dec	Gary Stuart Hocking (b. 30th September 1937) - Grand Prix motorcycle racing world champion (1961, 350cc and 500cc).
28th Dec	Ethel Carnie Holdsworth (b. 1st January 1886) - Working-class writer, feminist and socialist activist. *NB: Carnie Holdsworth was the first working-class woman in Britain to publish a novel.*

1962 TOP 10 SINGLES

Acker Bilk	No.1	Stranger On The Shore
Frank Ifield	No.2	I Remember You
The Shadows	No.3	Wonderful Land
Cliff Richard	No.4	The Young Ones
Elvis Presley	No.5	Can't Help Falling In Love
The Tornados	No.6	Telstar
Elvis Presley	No.7	Good Luck Charm
Chubby Checker	No.8	Let's Twist Again
Frank Ifield	No.9	Lovesick Blues
Ray Charles	No.10	I Can't Stop Lovin' You

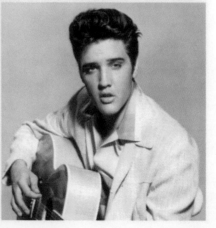

① Acker Bilk
Stranger On The Shore

Label:	Written by:	Length:
Columbia	Acker Bilk	2 mins 47 secs

Bernard Stanley Bilk, MBE (b. 28th January 1929 - d. 2nd November 2014) was clarinettist and vocalist known for his breathy, vibrato-rich, lower-register style, and distinctive appearance. Bilk's instrumental tune "Stranger On The Shore" was enormously successful and was the biggest selling record of 1962 in both the United Kingdom and the United States; it was also notably the first British recording to reach No.1 on the U.S. Billboard Hot 100.

---

② Frank Ifield
I Remember You

Label:	Written by:	Length:
Columbia	Mercer / Schertzinger	2 mins 4 secs

Francis Edward Ifield, OAM (b. 30th November 1937) is an English-Australian country music singer and guitarist who often incorporated yodelling into his songs. Born in Warwickshire, England, Ifield spent his formative years in Australia before returning to the United Kingdom in November 1959 where he had four No.1 hits in the British Singles Chart. The first of these was his cover version of Victor Schertzinger and Johnny Mercer's 1941 composition, "I Remember You", which topped the charts for seven weeks in May 1962.

3 The Shadows
Wonderful Land

Label:	Written by:	Length:
Columbia	Jerry Lordan	2 mins 5 secs

The Shadows (originally known as the Drifters) were an instrumental rock group. They were Cliff Richard's backing band from 1958 to 1968, and during their career placed 69 singles in the U.K. charts (35 credited to the Shadows, and 34 to Cliff Richard and the Shadows). They are the fifth most successful act in the British chart history behind Elvis Presley, the Beatles, Cliff Richard and Madonna.

---

4 Cliff Richard
The Young Ones

Label:	Written by:	Length:
Columbia	Tepper / Bennett	3 mins

Sir **Cliff Richard**, OBE (b. Harry Rodger Webb; 14th October 1940) is a pop singer, musician, performer, actor and philanthropist who has sold over 21 million singles in the U.K. and over 250 million records worldwide. "The Young Ones" is the title song to the 1961 film The Young Ones and its soundtrack album. With advance orders of over 500,000, it was released in January 1962 and went straight to No.1 in the charts, the first British single to do so since Elvis Presley's "It's Now Or Never" in November 1960.

5 Elvis Presley
Can't Help Falling In Love

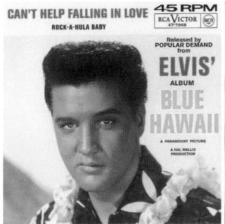 

Label:	Written by:	Length:
RCA	Weiss / Peretti / Creatore	2 mins 59 secs

Elvis Aaron Presley (b. 8th January 1935 - d. 16th August 1977) was a singer and actor. Regarded as one of the most significant cultural icons and influential musicians of the 20th century, he is often referred to as the King of Rock and Roll, or simply, the King. "Can't Help Falling In Love", which featured in Presley's 1961 film Blue Hawaii, topped the British charts in February 1962, spending four weeks at No.1.

---

6 The Tornados
Telstar

Label:	Written by:	Length:
Decca	Joe Meek	3 mins 15 secs

The Tornados were an instrumental group that acted as a backing band for many of record producer Joe Meek's productions and also for singer Billy Fury. They enjoyed several chart hits in their own right including the U.K. and U.S. No.1 "Telstar" (named after the satellite); "Telstar" was the first U.S. No.1 single by a British group.

7 **Elvis Presley**
Good Luck Charm

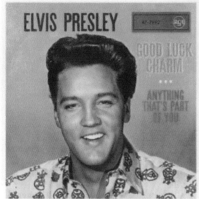  

Label:	Written by:	Length:
RCA	Schroeder / Gold	2 mins 23 secs

Good Luck Charm was recorded in Nashville, Tennessee, on the 15th October 1961. It reached the No.1 spot in the U.K. Singles Chart in May 1962, and stayed there for five weeks. Elvis Presley was commercially successful in many genres, including pop, blues and gospel, He is the best-selling solo artist in the history of recorded music with estimated record sales in excess 600 million units worldwide. He won three Grammys and also received the Grammy Lifetime Achievement Award at the age of 36.

---

8 **Chubby Checker**
Let's Twist Again

Label:	Written by:	Length:
Columbia	Appell / Mann	2 mins 16 secs

Chubby Checker (b. Ernest Evans; 3rd October 1941) is a rock and roll singer and dancer who is widely known for popularising many dance styles including the Twist and the Pony. His best-known song is the hit "Let's Twist Again" which refers to the Twist dance craze and Checker's 1960 single "The Twist" (a two-time U.S. No.1 single). *NB: In September 2008 "The Twist" was named the biggest chart hit of all time by Billboard magazine after reviewing all the singles that had made the charts between 1958 and 2008.*

⑨ Frank Ifield
Lovesick Blues

Label:	Written by:	Length:
Columbia	Friend / Mills	2 mins 17 secs

Lovesick Blues, a show tune written in 1922 by Cliff Friend and Irving Mills, was Frank Ifield's second British No.1 record. Although several cover versions of the song have been recorded over the years, Ifield's 1962 version is the most popular. In recognition of his contribution to music Frank Ifield was inducted into the Australian Roll of Renown in 2003, and the ARIA Hall of Fame in 2007.

---

⑩ Ray Charles
I Can't Stop Lovin' You

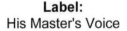

Label:	Written by:	Length:
His Master's Voice	Don Gibson	2 mins 37 secs

Ray Charles Robinson (b. 23rd September 1930 - d. 10th June 2004) was a singer, songwriter, pianist and composer who was blinded during childhood due to glaucoma. Often referred to as "the Genius" he won 18 Grammy Awards (including the Grammy Lifetime Achievement Award in 1987) during his near 60-year career. "I Can't Stop Loving You" reached No.1 in the U.K. Singles Chart in July 1962 and was Charles' first and only British No.1 recording.

1962: TOP FILMS

1. **Lawrence of Arabia** - *Columbia Pictures*
2. **To Kill a Mockingbird** - *Universal Pictures*
3. **The Music Man** - *Warner Bros.*
4. **The Longest Day** - *20th Century Fox*
5. **How the West Was Won** - *Metro-Goldwyn-Mayer*

OSCARS

Best Picture: Lawrence of Arabia

Most Nominations: Lawrence of Arabia (10)
Most Wins: Lawrence of Arabia (7)

Gregory Peck, Patty Duke, Joan Crawford (for Anne Bancroft) and Ed Begley.

Best Director: David Lean - *Lawrence of Arabia*

Best Actor: Gregory Peck - *To Kill a Mockingbird*
Best Actress: Anne Bancroft - *The Miracle Worker*
Best Supporting Actor: Ed Begley - *Sweet Bird of Youth*
Best Supporting Actress: Patty Duke - *The Miracle Worker*

The 35th Academy Awards, honouring the best in film for 1962, were presented on the 8th April 1963 at the Santa Monica Civic Auditorium in Santa Monica, California.

LAWRENCE OF ARABIA

Directed by: David Lean - Runtime: 3h 48min

The story of T.E. Lawrence, the English officer who successfully united and led the diverse, often warring, Arab tribes during World War I in order to fight the Turks.

Starring

Peter O'Toole
b. 2nd August 1932
d. 14th December 2013
Character:
Lawrence

Alec Guinness
b. 2nd April 1914
d. 5th August 2000
Character:
Prince Faisal

Anthony Quinn
b. 21st April 1915
d. 3rd June 2001
Character:
Auda Abu Tayi

Trivia

Goofs	The planes used during the air raid were DH Tiger Moths - they did not go into production until late 1929, early 1930. When Lawrence arrives at the Suez Canal the ship which comes into focus is a late-1950s Blue Funnel Line ship.
Interesting Facts	King Hussein of Jordan lent an entire brigade of his Arab Legion as extras for the film and frequently visited the set. During this time, Hussein became enamoured with a young British secretarial assistant working on the film, Antoinette Gardiner. She became Hussein's second wife; their eldest son, Abdullah, ascended to the throne and became King Abdullah II of Jordan in 1999. At 3 hours and 48 minutes in length, Lawrence of Arabia is reportedly the longest film ever made not to feature any dialogue spoken by a woman. The town of Aqaba was re-created in a dried river bed in southern Spain and consisted of over three hundred buildings. The film missed out on an eleventh Oscar nomination, for Best Costume Design, because someone forgot to submit Phyllis Dalton's name for consideration.
Quote	**Club Secretary**: I say, Lawrence. You are a clown! **T.E. Lawrence**: Ah, well, we can't all be lion tamers.

TO KILL A MOCKINGBIRD

Directed by: Robert Mulligan - Runtime: 2h 9min

Atticus Finch, a lawyer in the Depression-era South, defends a black man against an undeserved rape charge, and his children against prejudice.

Starring

Gregory Peck
b. 5th April 1916
d. 12th June 2003
Character:
Atticus Finch

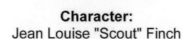

Mary Badham
b. 7th October 1952

Character:
Jean Louise "Scout" Finch

Phillip Alford
b. 11th September 1948

Character:
Jem Finch

Trivia

Goof | The "melon" Crayola crayon shown in the opening sequence was not introduced until 1949. The film is set in 1932.

Interesting Facts | After being offered the role of Atticus Finch, Gregory Peck quickly read Harper Lee's novel in one sitting and called director Robert Mulligan immediately afterwards to say that he would gladly play it.

The watch used in the film was a prop, but Harper Lee gave Gregory Peck her father's watch after the film was completed because he reminded her so much of him. *Fun fact: Gregory Peck's grandson Harper Peck Voll was named after Harper Lee.*

Mary Badham, who was nine years old during filming, became the youngest girl to receive an Oscar nomination (for Best Actress in a Supporting Role), coincidentally losing the award to another child actress, Patty Duke, aged fourteen, for The Miracle Worker (1962).

Mary Badham and Gregory Peck became close during filming and they kept in contact for all of Peck's life. Peck always called her "Scout", her character role, while Badham called Peck "Atticus".

Quote | **Atticus Finch:** If you just learn a single trick, Scout, you'll get along a lot better with all kinds of folks. You never really understand a person until you consider things from his point of view... until you climb inside of his skin and walk around in it.

THE MUSIC MAN

Directed by: Morton DaCosta - Runtime: 2h 31min

Travelling con man Harold Hill tries to convince naive Iowa townsfolk to start a band by purchasing the uniforms and instruments from him.

Starring

Robert Preston
b. 8th June 1918
d. 21st March 1987
Character:
Harold Hill

Shirley Jones
b. 31st March 1934
Character:
Marian Paroo

Buddy Hackett
b. 31st August 1924
d. 30th June 2003
Character:
Marcellus Washburn

Trivia

Goof | Set in 1912, the song "Ya Got Trouble" mentions both the beverage Bevo (first offered in 1916) and the magazine "Captain Billy's Whiz-Bang" (first published in 1919).

Interesting Facts | The Broadway play, on which the film is based, opened in 1957 to critical acclaim and huge box office success. Its run lasted five years and included 1,375 performances. The Music Man was nominated for eight Tony awards and won five for 1957, including the Tony for best musical (defeating Jerome Robbins' West Side Story).

In an early episode of the TV series Happy Days (1974), Howard and Marion Cunningham are coming out of a cinema when they pause in the lobby and look at the poster for The Music Man. Marion comments how much the little boy in the film (Winthrop) "looks so much like Richie did when he was little". Both Winthrop and Richie were played by Ron Howard.

Two songs in the film "76 Trombones" and "Good Night My Someone" are the same tune, played in different tempos. Meredith Willson used this technique to present a masculine and feminine slant on the on the events surrounding Harold Hill's arrival in River City and his budding relationship with Marian.

Quote | **Marian Paroo**: No, please, not tonight. Maybe tomorrow.
Harold Hill: Oh, my dear little librarian. You pile up enough tomorrows, and you'll find you've collected nothing but a lot of empty yesterdays. I don't know about you, but I'd like to make today worth remembering.

THE LONGEST DAY

Directed by: Ken Annakin / Andrew Marton / Bernhard Wicki - Runtime: 2h 58min

The events of the D-Day invasion of Normandy in WWII told on a grand scale from both the Allied and German points of view.

Starring

John Wayne

b. 26th May 1907
d. 11th June 1979
Character:
Lt. Col. Benjamin
Vandervoort

Henry Fonda

b. 16th May 1905
d. 12th August 1982
Character:
Brig. Gen. Theodore
Roosevelt Jr.

Robert Mitchum

b. 6th August 1917
d. 1st July 1997
Character:
Brig. Gen. Norman Cota

Trivia

Goofs	The first time we encounter Field Marshal Erwin Rommel (Werner Hinz) in the film he is talking about how calm and peaceful the sea between French coast and England looks. As he walks to the center of the screen he suddenly disappears before magically reappearing around five seconds later.
	After scaling the cliffs there is a scene where three soldiers run past a German who throws a grenade. The grenade explodes at one of the soldiers' feet but he continues running as if nothing has happened.
Interesting Facts	Lt. Col. Benjamin Vandevoort was 27 years old on D-Day. He was very disappointed to find that he was being played by the 54-year-old John Wayne. Wayne was generally considered too old and overweight to play a paratrooper in his twenties.
	While clearing a section of the Normandy beach near Ponte du Hoc the crew unearthed a tank that had been buried in the sand since the original invasion. Mechanics cleaned it off, fixed it up, and it was used in the film as part of the British tank regiment.
	With a $10-million budget, this was the most expensive black-and-white film ever made until Schindler's List (1993).
Quote	**Maj. Werner Pluskat**: *[on the phone]* You know those five thousand ships you say the Allies haven't got? Well, they've got them!

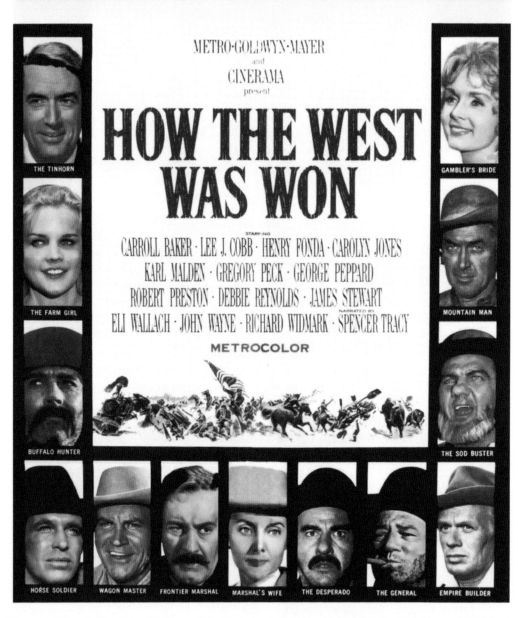

Directed by: John Ford / Henry Hathaway / George Marshall - Runtime: 2h 44min

Fifty years of American westward expansion as viewed through the experiences of the Prescott family.

Starring

Carroll Baker
b. 28ᵗʰ May 1931

Character:
Eve Prescott

Lee J. Cobb
b. 8ᵗʰ December 1911
d. 11ᵗʰ February 1976
Character:
Marshal Lou Ramsey

Henry Fonda
b. 16ᵗʰ May 1905
d. 12ᵗʰ August 1982
Character:
Jethro Stuart

Trivia

Goofs | When the wagon train, on its way to California, is attacked by Indians it is in a mountainous area, yet the Indians are identified as Cheyenne. The Cheyenne tribe was a Great Plains tribe and would not have been that far west.

Ma and Pa Prescott are buried on the bank of the river in which they drowned. When Eve visits her parent's graves decades later there is no sign of a river anywhere nearby.

Interesting Facts | Of the films' five segments, covering 1839 to 1889, Henry Hathaway directed The Rivers, The Plains and The Outlaws, John Ford directed The Civil War and George Marshall The Railroad. Some uncredited work was done by Richard Thorpe.

John Ford's habit was to always sit beside the camera while it was filming so he could watch the action intently. Unfortunately, because of the triple lens on the Cinerama camera he kept appearing in shots. To overcome this director of photography Joseph LaShelle hit on the idea of building a rig that allowed Ford to sit above the camera.

Spencer Tracy was only able to narrate the film rather than play a part due to his poor health problems.

Quote | **Cleve Van Valen**: From the first moment I saw you I've known that I couldn't live without you.
Lilith Prescott: Well... I'd hate to be the cause of your death, Mr. Van Valen.

SPORTING WINNERS

BBC SPORTS PERSONALITY OF THE YEAR

1962	BBC Sports Personality Results	Country	Sport
Winner	**Anita Lonsbrough**	**England**	**Swimming**
Runner Up	Dorothy Hyman	England	Athletics
Third Place	Linda Ludgrove	England	Swimming

Anita Lonsbrough - Swimming

Anita Lonsbrough, MBE (b. 10th August 1941), later known by her married name Anita Porter, is a former swimmer who won her first gold medal for swimming in the 1958 British Empire and Commonwealth Games. Five world records and seven gold medals followed until her retirement in 1964.

Gold Medals:

Year	Competition	Event	Location
1958	British Empire & Commonwealth Games	200yd breaststroke	Cardiff
1958	British Empire & Commonwealth Games	4×110yd medley	Cardiff
1960	Olympic Games	200m breaststroke	Rome
1962	European Championships	200m breaststroke	Leipzig
1962	British Empire & Commonwealth Games	110yd breaststroke	Perth
1962	British Empire & Commonwealth Games	220yd breaststroke	Perth
1962	British Empire & Commonwealth Games	440yd individual medley	Perth

Lonsbrough was the first female flag bearer for Great Britain at the 1964 Summer Olympics, and the first woman winner of BBC Sports Personality of the Year. She was inducted into the International Swimming Hall of Fame in 1983.

FIVE NATIONS RUGBY CHAMPIONSHIP - FRANCE

Position	Nation	Played	Won	Draw	Lost	For	Against	+/-	Points
1st	**France**	4	3	0	1	35	6	+29	6
2nd	Wales	4	2	1	1	34	23	+11	5
3rd	Scotland	4	1	2	1	19	16	+3	4
4th	England	4	1	2	1	9	11	-2	4
5th	Ireland	4	0	1	3	9	50	-41	1

The 1962 Five Nations Championship was the thirty-third series of the rugby union Five Nations Championship. Including the previous incarnations as the Home Nations and Five Nations, this was the sixty-eighth series of the northern hemisphere rugby union championship. Contested by England, France, Ireland, Scotland and Wales, ten matches were played between the 13th January and the 17th November 1962.

Date	Team		Score		Team	Location
13-01-1962	Scotland		3-11		France	Edinburgh
20-01-1962	England		0-0		Wales	London
03-02-1962	Wales		3-8		Scotland	Cardiff
10-02-1962	England		16-0		Ireland	London
24-02-1962	France		13-0		England	Paris
24-02-1962	Ireland		6-20		Scotland	Dublin
17-03-1962	Scotland		3-3		England	Edinburgh
24-03-1962	Wales		3-0		France	Cardiff
14-04-1962	France		11-0		Ireland	Paris
17-11-1962	Ireland		3-3		Wales	Dublin

CALCUTTA CUP

ENGLAND ➕ 3-3 ✖ SCOTLAND

The Calcutta Cup was first awarded in 1879 and is the rugby union trophy awarded to the winner of the match (currently played as part of the Six Nations Championship) between England and Scotland. The Cup was presented to the Rugby Football Union after the Calcutta Football Club in India disbanded in 1878. It is made from melted down silver rupees withdrawn from the club's funds.

Historical Records	England	Scotland	Draws
	71 Wins	41 Wins	16

BRITISH GRAND PRIX - JIM CLARK

Jim Clark in his Lotus 25 Climax at the 1962 British Grand Prix.

The 1962 British Grand Prix was a Formula One motor race held on the 21st July at the Aintree Motor Racing Circuit near Liverpool. The race was won by Scotsman Jim Clark, from pole position, over 75 laps of the 3-mile circuit. John Surtees and Bruce McLaren took second and third places respectively.

1962 GRAND PRIX SEASON

Date	Grand Prix	Circuit	Winning Driver	Constructor
20-05	Dutch	Zandvoort	Graham Hill	BRM
03-06	Monaco	Monaco	Bruce McLaren	Cooper-Climax
17-06	Belgian	Spa-Francorchamps	Jim Clark	Lotus-Climax
08-07	French	Rouen-Les-Essarts	Dan Gurney	Porsche
21-07	British	Aintree	Jim Clark	Lotus-Climax
05-08	German	Nürburgring	Graham Hill	BRM
16-09	Italian	Monza	Graham Hill	BRM
07-10	United States	Watkins Glen	Jim Clark	Lotus-Climax
29-12	South African	Prince George	Graham Hill	BRM

The 1962 Formula One season was the 16th season of the FIA's Formula One motor racing. It featured the 1962 World Championship of Drivers which was contested over 9 races and was won by Graham Hill with 42 points; Jim Clark was second with 30 points and Bruce McLaren third with 27 points. The season also featured the 1962 International Cup for F1 Manufacturers which was won by British Racing Motors (BRM).

GRAND NATIONAL - KILMORE

The 1962 Grand National was the 116th renewal of this world famous horse race and took place at Aintree Racecourse near Liverpool on the 31st March. Kilmore, ridden by jockey Fred Winter and trained by Ryan Price, won the race by 10 lengths.

Of the 32 horses that contested the race 17 finished; 6 fell, 6 pulled up, 2 unseated their riders and 1 was brought down. All thirty-two horses returned safely to the stables.

Photo: Kilmore being led into the winners' enclosure after winning the 1962 Grand National at Aintree.

	Horse	Jockey	Age	Weight	Odds
1st	**Kilmore**	**Fred Winter**	**12**	**10st-4lb**	**28/1**
2nd	Wyndburgh	Tommy Barnes	12	10st-9lb	45/1
3rd	Mr What	Johnny Lehane	12	10st-9lb	22/1
4th	Gay Navaree	Tony Cameron	10	10st-0lb	100/1
5th	Fredith's Son	Francis Shortt	11	10st-11lb	66/1

EPSOM DERBY - LARKSPUR

The Derby Stakes is Britain's richest horse race and the most prestigious of the country's five Classics. First run in 1780 this Group 1 flat horse race is open to 3-year-old thoroughbred colts and fillies. The race takes place at Epsom Downs in Surrey over a distance of one mile, four furlongs and 10 yards (2,423 metres) and is scheduled for early June each year.

Photo: Irish-bred, American-owned Thoroughbred racehorse and sire Larkspur (foaled January 1959) crosses the line to win the 1962 Epsom Derby. The horse was owned by Raymond R. Guest, trained by Vincent O'Brien and ridden by jockey Neville Sellwood.

FOOTBALL LEAGUE CHAMPIONS

England:

Pos.	Team	W	D	L	F	A	Pts.
1	**Ipswich Town**	**24**	**8**	**10**	**93**	**67**	**56**
2	Burnley	21	11	10	101	67	53
3	Tottenham Hotspur	21	10	11	88	69	52
4	Everton	20	11	11	88	54	51
5	Sheffield United	19	9	14	61	69	47

Scotland:

Pos.	Team	W	D	L	F	A	Pts.
1	**Dundee**	**25**	**4**	**5**	**80**	**46**	**54**
2	Rangers	22	7	5	84	31	51
3	Celtic	19	8	7	81	37	46
4	Dunfermline Athletic	19	5	10	77	46	43
5	Kilmarnock	16	10	8	74	58	42

FA CUP WINNERS - TOTTENHAM HOTSPUR

Tottenham Hotspur   3-1   Burnley

The 1962 FA Cup Final took place on the 5th May at Wembley Stadium in front of 100,000 fans. Tottenham Hotspur won the match 3-1 in what was the last final with exposed terraces at Wembley; by 1963 the roof had been extended all the way around the stadium in preparation for the 1966 FIFA World Cup. *Photo: Tottenham players (left to right) Ron Henry, Cliff Jones, Dave Mackay, Jimmy Greaves, Maurice Norman and goalkeeper Bill Brown celebrating after winning the FA Cup for the second year running.*

County Championship Cricket - Yorkshire

The 1962 County Championship was the 63rd officially organised running of this cricket competition and saw Yorkshire win their 25th Championship title.

Pos.	Team	Pld.	Won	Lost	Drawn	No Decision	Bonus	Points	Avg.
1	**Yorkshire**	**32**	**14**	**4**	**14**	**0**	**36**	**224**	**7.00**
2	Worcestershire	32	14	3	14	1	34	220	6.87
3	Warwickshire	32	12	5	15	0	32	202	6.31
4	Gloucestershire	28	11	11	6	0	24	174	6.21
5	Surrey	28	10	3	14	1	32	174	6.21

England Vs Pakistan Test Series

England 4-0 Pakistan

Test	Dates	Ground	Result
1st	31/05 - 04/06	Edgbaston, Birmingham	England won by an innings and 24 runs
2nd	21/06 - 23/06	Lord's, London	England won by 9 wickets
3rd	05/07 - 07/07	Headingley, Leeds	England won by an innings and 117 runs
4th	26/07 - 31/07	Trent Bridge, Nottingham	Match drawn
5th	16/08 - 20/08	The Oval, London	England won by 10 wickets

Golf Open Championship Arnold Palmer

The 1962 Open Championship was the 91st to be played and was held between the 11th and 13th of July at Troon Golf Club in Troon, Scotland. Arnold Palmer won his second consecutive Open (six strokes ahead of runner-up Kel Nagle) to take the sixth of his seven major titles and £1,400 in prize money.

Photo: Arnold Palmer at the Firestone Country Club in Akron, Ohio (1962).

WIMBLEDON

Photos: Rod Laver and Karen Susman holding aloft their Championship trophies.

Men's Singles Champion: Rod Laver - Australia
Ladies Singles Champion: Karen Susman - United States

The 1962 Wimbledon Championships was the 76th staging of tournament and took place on the outdoor grass courts at the All England Lawn Tennis and Croquet Club in Wimbledon, London. It ran from the 25th June until the 7th July and was the third Grand Slam tennis event of 1962.

Men's Singles Final:

Country	Player	Set 1	Set 2	Set 3
Australia	Rod Laver	6	6	6
Australia	Martin Mulligan	2	2	1

Women's Singles Final:

Country	Player	Set 1	Set 2
United States	Karen Susman	6	6
Czechoslovakia	Věra Suková	4	4

Men's Doubles Final:

Country	Players	Set 1	Set 2	Set 3	Set 4
Australia	Bob Hewitt / Fred Stolle	6	5	6	6
Yugoslavia	Boro Jovanović / Nikola Pilić	2	7	2	4

Women's Doubles Final:

Country	Players	Set 1	Set 2	Set 3
United States	Billie Jean Moffitt / Karen Susman	5	6	7
South Africa	Sandra Price / Renée Schuurman	7	3	5

Mixed Doubles Final:

Country	Players	Set 1	Set 2	Set 3
Australia / United States	Neale Fraser / Margaret duPont	2	6	13
United States / United Kingdom	Dennis Ralston / Ann Haydon	6	3	11

COST OF LIVING

AN IMPORTANT

ANNOUNCEMENT

Introducing

Cow&Gate

DAIRY WEANING FOODS

6OZ. TINS FOR ONLY 9d (from all Chemists)

COW & GATE

The choice of millions of mothers

Comparison Chart

	1962	1962 (+ Inflation)	2021	% Change
3 Bedroom House	£4,100	£92,178	£235,243	+155.2%
Weekly Income	£9.1s.1d	£203.56	£621	+205.1%
Pint Of Beer	1s.2d	£1.31	£3.94	+200.1%
Cheese (lb)	3s.6d	£3.93	£3.04	-22.6%
Bacon (lb)	4s.4d	£4.87	£3.20	-34.3%
The Beano	3d	28p	£2.75	+882.1%

Clothes

Women's Clothing

Harrod's Spring Coat	38gns
Sugden's Beaver Lamb Fur Coat	19gns
Fairway House Summer Duster Coat	£1.9s.6d
Pringle Thornton Lambswool Sweater	£9.19s.6d
Marshall & Snelgrove Pure Silk Print Dress	19gns
David Gibson Peppermint Stripe Dress	7½gns
Hardy Amies Lido Maternity Dress	£4.9s.6d
Fairy Ring Cross-Over Blouse	£3.3s
Weargood Cavalry Twill Slacks	£2.2s.6d
Fantasie Corselette	£7.19s.6d
Fantasie Deep Bra	£2.19s.6d
Alstons Hugger Corset	£3.9s
Locknit Slip (x2)	19s.11d
Fairway House Cellular Briefs (x6)	9s.11d
Marshall Ward Alpine Leisure Bootees	£2.7s.6d

FANTASIE

Fantasie foundations of breathtaking loveliness fashioned in the new wonder fabric 'Vyrene' containing no rubber at all.

FANTASIE Corselette C1650 in Vyrene Jacquard with Vyrene satin downstretch back. Swiss embroidered Nylon voile front and bust sections. Plush lined shoulder straps. White only. B cup fittings, sizes 34″ to 40″.

£7.19.6

post free

FANTASIE Girdle G4710. An elegant high waist girdle in Vyrene Jacquard with Vyrene satin downstretch back. Swiss embroidered Nylon voile front panel. Side zip. White only. Tailored waist sizes 26″ to 34″.

£6.9.6

post free

FANTASIE Deep Bra B2600, ensuring perfect diaphragm control. Vyrene Jacquard with bust sections and diaphragm of Swiss embroidered Nylon voile. White only. B Cup fittings, sizes 32″ to 38″. C cup fittings, sizes 34″ to 40″.

59/6

post free

Delightful duet
by Pringle

... proving irresistibly that two Pringles
are better than one. And even one
Pringle is always a joy in itself. Sweaters
in softest Spindrift lambswool
team flawlessly with dyed-to-match skirts.

DARVEL Sleek collarless jacket doubles with a fully-lined
straight skirt for easy elegance. Price: £10.19.6.

THORNTON Lambswool sweater with a middy neckline
gaily partners a tailored and lined skirt. Price: £9.19.6.
Four new shades for Spring: Crayon Blue, Pineapple, Caramel,
Linden Green.

PRINGLE OF SCOTLAND LTD · HAWICK

Men's Clothing

Showerproofed Gaberdine Raincoat	£6.14s.6d
Pure Wool Duffle Jacket	£1.2s.6d
Yorkshire Tweed Sports Jacket	£3.9s.6d
Terylene / Wool Solid Worsted Suit	£9.4s.6d
Sports Slacks	£1.17s.6d
Bonny Clad Suede Finish Casual Shoes	15s.6ds
Montfort Airlift Nylon Mesh Socks	3s.11d

Electrical Items

Hotpoint F50 Refrigerator	59gns
Hotpoint Supermatic Twin Tub	84gns
19in Astra Mark II B&W Television	66gns
Murphy Stereophonic Radiogram	£72.7s.5d
Stereo Ready Record Player	24gns
Super Tone 4-Transistor Tape Recorder	£4.19s.6d
The 200 Special Transistor Pocket Radio Receiver	£8.19s.6d
Bell Music 'Holborn' Solid Body Electric Guitar	£6.19s.6d
8mm Electric Zoom Projector	27½gns
Electric Driven 8mm Rexina Cine Camera	£9.19s.6d
Sofono Jupiter Wall-Mounted Infra-Red Heater	£5.14s.6d
2 Bar Coal Effect Electric Fire	£4.19s.6d
Philips Phantom Fan Heater	£9.2s.2d
Hi-Speed Electric Kettle	£4.10s

Various Other Items & Their Cost

Belgravia 3-Bedroom Maisonette S.W.1	£10,750
Vauxhall Cresta Car	£918.17.11d
Wolseley 1500 Car	£774.3s.1d
M.G. Midget Car	£689.9s.6d
Weeks Popular Plus 4½-Ton Trailer	£162.10s
Radio Rentals 19" Television (per week)	8s.6d
Caronia 92 Day World Cruise (23 ports)	£1018
14 Day Holiday Majorca (inc. flight)	40gns
13 Day Rimini & Venice Coach Tour	27½gns
10 Day Austrian Tyrol Coach Tour	19gns
8 Day Cosmos Tour Paris (air / coach)	13gns
1 Week Prestatyn Holiday Camp Wales	£8.15s
Channel Islands Return Flights	£5.12s
Marshall & Snelgrove Double Divan Bed	£57.7s.6d
2-Tier Bunk Beds	£2.5s
Denhill Skymaster 17x50 Binoculars	15gns
Viscount 35mm Colour Camera	£7
21 Jewel Razor Edge Automatic Watch	£6.15s
Swiss 15 Jewel Ladies Waterproof Watch	£5.5s
Johnnie Walker Whisky	£2.1s.6d
Bisquit 3-Star Cognac Brandy	£2.8s.6d
Booth's Finest Dry Gin	£1.19s.9d
RSVP Cream Sherry	8s
VP Cherry Wine	7s.9d
Babycham (24 bottle case)	£1.16s
Players No.3 Cigarettes (50)	12s.3½d
Du Maurier Cigarettes (20)	4s.6d
Woman's Own Magazine	6d
Daily Mirror Newspaper	3d

Money Conversion Table

Pounds / Shillings / Pence 1962 'Old Money'		Decimal Value	Value 2021 (Rounded)
Farthing	¼d	0.1p	2p
Half Penny	½d	0.21p	5p
Penny	1d	0.42p	9p
Threepence	3d	1.25p	28p
Sixpence	6d	2.5p	56p
Shilling	1s	5p	£1.12
Florin	2s	10p	£2.25
Half Crown	2s.6d	12.5p	£2.81
Crown	5s	25p	£5.62
Ten Shillings	10s	50p	£11.24
Pound	20s	£1	£22.48
Guinea	21s	£1.05	£23.61
Five Pounds	£5	£5	£112.41
Ten Pounds	£10	£10	£224.82

FLY AWAY

FAR AWAY

£539.10s.* buys you a slice of South America!

*25-day inclusive tour, flying BOAC

All over the world **B·O·A·C** takes good care of you

BRITISH OVERSEAS AIRWAYS CORPORATION

The spacious new six–cylinder
VAUXHALL
VELOX | CRESTA
£680 +£142.4.7 P.T.
Total £822.4.7 | £760 +£158.17.11 P.T.
Total £918.17.11

1½ litre performance
and **W**OLSELEY luxury
for only £774.3.1 (inc. P.T.)

The compact lively economical
WOLSELEY
1500 FIFTEEN HUNDRED

WOLSELEY-A LUXURIOUS WAY OF MOTORING